Old 'Derry

by **John Hanna**

A ship discharging its cargo alongside 'Derry Quay. Each bag of cargo was lifted to the side of the ship on a small truck and then slid down the board to workers on the quayside. The port was a centre for the importation and export of potatoes and at one time all Cyprus potatoes coming into Ireland came through the port. Steamboats commenced freight and passenger services between the port and Glasgow in 1825 and these were maintained until 1966. In 1963 as many as 500 dock labourers worked in the port.

Text © John Hanna, 2008
First published in the United Kingdom, 2008,
by Stenlake Publishing Ltd.
www.stenlake.co.uk
ISBN 9781840334265

The publishers regret that they cannot supply copies of any pictures featured in this book.

In this view of the city wharves several small coal-burning coastal vessels are moored alongside where a steam crane is being used to unload the nearest ship. The other ship has a 'K' on its funnel which may denote that it is a Kelly coal boat from Belfast. In 1615 the Irish Society built a wharf at Londonderry, thereby increasing trade. There were ferries crossing the river at this time and the two pence fare remained the same right up to 1940. Leaving the wharf is one of three ferries which operated different routes: Guildhall to Midland Railway Station; Abercorn Quay to Midland Railway Station: and Guildhall to Ebrington Barracks. The ferries were named *Roe*, *Foyle* and *S M Alexander*.

Acknowledgements

The author would like to thank the following for their help: the most helpful and willing staff at 'Derry Central Library, and Mr Richard Doherty. The publishers wish to thank Des Quail for contributing the photographs on the inside front cover, pages 9, 10 (left), 16 (right), 17, 21, 24, 27, 30, 33, 37, 38, 42, 45-47, the inside back cover and the back cover.

Further reading

The books listed were used by the author during his research. None of them is available from Stenlake Publishing. Those interested in finding out more are advised to contact their local bookshop or reference library.

David Bigger and Terence McDonald, *In Sunshine or in Shadow*, Friar's Bush Press, 1990.
S. Cooke, *The Maiden City and the Western Ocean*, Morris and Company, 1979.
Philip Cunningham, *Derry Down the Day*, Guildhall Press, 2002.
Roy Hamilton, *100 Years of Derry*, Blackstaff Press, 1999.
Brian Lacey, Siege City, *The Story of Londonderry and Derry*, Blackstaff Press, 1990.

INTRODUCTION

Londonderry, to give it its official name, is the second city of Ulster and probably its most historic place. It is situated in the north-west of the Province at the head of Lough Foyle. Originally named and, more recently, popularly called 'Derry, it took its name from the Irish *Doire* which translated means 'a place of oaks'. There is evidence to prove the existence of a farming community here as long ago as 4000 BC, however the city owes its beginning to the founding of an abbey in AD 546 by St Columba on an island in the River Foyle. This settlement soon became a trading community and as such was the target for many attackers both from within Ireland and Scandinavia. In AD 983 the shrine of St Columba was carried away by the Danes and they devastated the site on a number of occasions around the end of the tenth century.

By the middle ages the town was thriving and the Great Church (Tempull Mor) was built. By now 'Derry was no longer an island as the western arm of the river had dried up and the marshy area left behind became known as the Bogside. At the start of the fourteenth century the great church was destroyed by fire and no trace remains of it. For the next few hundred years the ecclesiastical centre was fought for by rival Irish Chieftains until the dominant O'Donnell renewed his oath of allegiance to King Henry VIII. After a rebellion by Shane O'Neill was defeated Sir Henry Docwra arrived with an English force of 4,000 foot and 200 horse. He obtained a charter and planted a colony but the O'Dohertys rebelled against the Crown and Sir Cahir O'Doherty seized 'Derry by force in 1608. He was easily defeated and a governor, Sir Arthur Chichester, was appointed in 1609. Around this time, King James I began the Plantation of Ulster, bringing Protestant settlers from Scotland and England and giving them lands confiscated from the local Catholics. The new settlers arrived in 1612 and were funded partly by the Guilds of the City of London. In the same year an agreement was made with the Corporation of London to rebuild the city, and the Irish Society was formed. The name of the new city was changed to Londonderry and the Society was to fortify the town and enclose it within stone walls. These were completed in 1618 and withstood two sieges in 1641 and 1649.

In 1688 Londonderry became a refuge for the Protestants of the north who were fleeing from the advancing Catholic forces of King James II. Some 30,000 people were within the walls when thirteen young apprentice boys closed the gates in the face of James's emissaries, and a siege began on 7 December 1688. It lasted 105 days and during that time many thousands of people died either from starvation or fighting for the defence of the city. On the 28 July 1689 the ship *Mountjoy* broke through the boom that had been placed across the river and the siege was relieved. Only 4,300 of the defenders survived.

In the eighteenth century the city was rebuilt, beginning a period of rapid growth. This expansion took place both outside the city walls and across the river. By the 1800s 'Derry was industrialised and had become an important centre for the production of linen. It had a thriving port and was one of Ireland's principal emigration ports. Its role changed dramatically with the Partition of Ireland in 1921 when it became a border city. This deprived it of trade with its natural hinterland in Donegal; this, combined with the general economic downturn of the 1930s, led to hard times. Its fortunes were restored with the outbreak of the Second World War when the port of Londonderry became one of the most important Allied harbours in Europe. With many American and Commonwealth servicemen based locally and spending money, the city was booming.

But the hard times returned in the post-war years and by the 1960s dissatisfaction was growing among the Catholic population. Civil rights were lacking, there was a great shortage of housing for the rapidly growing population, the four railway lines were closed, and there was gerrymandering in favour of the Unionist minority. Another issue was the downgrading of the city's Magee College in favour of the new University of Ulster which was built in the Unionist town of Coleraine. All of this culminated in the setting up of the Civil Rights Movement and the rising tension led to the outbreak of riots and the so-called 'Troubles' in 1968. The early 1970s were a disaster for the city and many of its fine buildings were destroyed. In fact, between 1970 and 1974 5,200 homes were destroyed or badly damaged, 124 business premises were destroyed and another 1,800 damaged. There was also a great loss of life.

The last two decades have seen a steady improvement and the city now has a vibrant campus for the University of Ulster. There is increased modern housing and new shopping centres. The port has moved downstream to the former naval base at Lisahally and is busy. Added to all this, the restoration and redevelopment of many buildings has transformed the look of the city and it is now attracting a large number of tourists. The future looks bright.

The Diamond, photographed prior to 1917. Originally it was named King Willam Square. The layout of the old city within the walls was of four main streets radiating out from the Diamond to the four original gates in the walls. Shipquay Street ran in a north-easterly direction, Bishop Street south-westerly, Butcher Street north-westerly and Ferryquay Street south-easterly. This layout still exists today. The Diamond's gardens were created after the Corporation Hall, which had stood on the site, was demolished in 1910. The statue is of Sir Robert Ferguson, 1795—1860, the city's MP from 1830 to 1860. Locally known as the 'black man', the statute was erected in 1863 but was moved to Brooke Park in 1927 as it impeded traffic flow in and out of Shipquay Street.

Ferryquay Gate as viewed from the intersection of Bridge Street, Carlisle Road and Orchard Street. To the right is the Victoria Hotel and Bars, advertising on the window 'Watts Tyrconnell Whisky'; to its left is a shop selling and repairing umbrellas. The Victoria Hotel was popular with the actresses and actors starring in the Opera House just down Carlisle Road. To the left, the rounded building belonged to Barr and McClement, outfitters, established in 1899. This building has been replaced by one of the same shape and the current tenants are Clockwork Orange. The two keystones on the gate are heads of George Walker and James Gordon, two leading figures in the siege of 1689. In 1995 the buildings on the right were demolished to make way for the entrance to the Foyleside shopping centre. It was this gate that was actually closed by the Apprentice Boys in the face of the Earl of Antrim's troops on 7 December 1688, thus beginning the siege.

Ferryquay Street as viewed from the Diamond and looking towards Ferryquay Gate. Originally called Gracious Street, the name was changed as the thoroughfare led to the ferry across the Foyle before the first bridge was built. Woolworth's opened their premises on this street (the second building on the left, counting back from the gate) just after the end of the First World War and remain there today, although they were rebuilt after being damaged in the 1970s. To the left, the brick building is the shop of Rosborough. To the right is the corner entrance to Austin's, describing themselves on the window as merchant tailors and outfitters. Further down the street, on the right, is Tyler's. The buildings on the left were demolished in 1984 to make way for the Richmond Centre.

Dominating the southern point of the Diamond is Austin & Co.'s department store. Presenting a conglomeration of large windows, columns, pedestals and balconies, and with a copper-covered cupola, this fine five-storey building was designed by M.A. Robinson and built in 1907. It was at that time the largest independent department store in Ireland. Austin's has been managed by the Hassan family since 1976. In the centre of the Diamond is the 'Derry War Memorial, built on the site of the Corporation Hall, and originally unfenced. The basement of the hall, which may have been a prison prior to 1784, has been retained underground.

Shipquay Street, formerly known as Silver Street, viewed from the Diamond and looking towards the Guildhall and Shipquay Gate. Shipquay Gate was built in 1805 and has on it the symbols of commerce illustrating the link between the heart of the city's business life and the commercial area of the quayside. These symbols are a cornucopia, a horn overflowing with fruit as a symbol of plenty, and a caduceus, a staff carried by the god Hermes to protect merchants. A 'bullnose' Morris is creating a lot of smoke on its way up the hill, which is perhaps not surprising as it is the steepest street in Ireland. The offices of the *Derry Standard* are on the left, and next door are those of the Royal Insurance Company. On the right is the office of the *Derry Journal*, which moved from the Diamond to the street in 1832. Most of the buildings on this street remain intact.

Bishop Gate was one of the four original gates in the city walls, although in 1879 it became the first gate to be rebuilt, to a design by Henry Aaron Baker of Dublin. The carved keystones and panels are by the sculptor Edward Smyth. On the outer side, seen here from Bishop Street, the keystone is of a head with a stern expression, crowned by the prow of a ship, which represents the River Boyne, 1690. On the inner side is a determined face crowned by a laurel wreath, representing the River Foyle. This was considered the weakest section of the defences and it was here that King James's forces tried to gain access to the city, but to no avail. To the right is the Arch Bar and a van from the Emerald Isle Confectionery Company of Ballymoney is making a delivery to a confectioner next door. On its side the van advertises 'Peggy's Leg', which was a local toffee. All the buildings seen here have been demolished; on the left-hand side, just beside the wall, there is now a small peace park.

Right: Butcher Gate looking into Butcher Street with the faint outline of the Corporation Hall in the Diamond in the background. Plainly designed, in comparison to Bishop Gate and Ferryquay Gate, this gate is named after the tanning industry that took place close by. Nowadays, just inside the gate to the left is the Tower Hotel, built in 1994.

Above: A view of Foyle Street close to Guildhall Square. The City Hotel is at the far end on the right while next to it is the smaller Provincial Hotel; the large building nearest on the right contains C. Porter, wholesale newsagents. On the left are the offices of the Canadian Pacific Railway Company which were later converted into the Criterion Hotel. The Melville Hotel was also close by.

Looking along Foyle Street towards the Guildhall, on the left are the premises of wine and spirit merchant B. McLaughlin, while next is A.D. Kennedy's general store, and then another public house owned by A. Doherty. There were many bed and breakfast hotels in this street and signs are hanging outside Grant's café and boarding accommodation and Ramsey's Central House. Further along on the left was Newton Buildings. The low arches to the right were the entrances to the Butter and Pork Market and the large gable belonged to the premises of J. and R. Roulston, wholesale importers of flour and feeding stuffs.

Opposite: A view looking south-west along Grand Parade towards the Walker Memorial Pillar. This area was used as a parade ground in the eighteenth century. The governor of Londonderry from December 1688 to 20 April 1689 was Colonel Lundy and, when the troops of King James II were trying to take the city, he tried to persuade the defenders to surrender. In the end he was forced to flee, disguised as an ordinary soldier. He was replaced as governor by the Reverend George Walker, Rector of Donoughmore in County Tyrone, who had come to 'Derry to assist the besieged citizens. The Walker Memorial Pillar was erected to his memory in 1828 at an expense of £12,000. The pillar was constructed of Portland stone in the Roman Doric Style with a statue of Walker on top. The design was by John Smith of Dublin, and it was possible to ascend the 81-foot column by a spiral staircase within. This was the site for the annual burning of an 18-foot effigy of Lundy, who was seen as a traitor. The Walker Memorial was destroyed by a bomb in 1972. The building behind the gates and lamps is the First Derry Presbyterian Church, which was revamped in 1903 with the Imperial Roman portico. There has been a Presbyterian congregation and church here since 1642; in recent years it has been vacant for some time but it is now to be refurbished so that the congregation can return. Further along the walls is the Apprentice Boys Memorial Hall, built in 1873 in the antiquarian baronial style to a design of John Grey Ferguson at a cost of £3,250. A further £3,000 was spent in extending the building along Society Street in 1937. More recently a memorial garden has been added and what remained of the statue of George Walker stands in it. Along this part of the walls 15 sycamore trees have been planted.

Right: Looking along the walls to Butcher Gate, the depth and width of the outside wall can be seen clearly and the original ditch outside the wall has been converted to a street, Nailor's Row – so named because of the presence of artisans making iron nails for the wooden ships being built by the river. The street led down to St Columb's well. Nos. 1 and 2 in Lower Nailor's Row was a house/shop owned by Johnny Larmour; it was said that he sold everything from needles to anchors, and he often displayed a wide variety of second-hand household goods up against the city walls. This area was demolished between 1947 and 1953 and replaced with Fahan Street.

A most interesting view, taken from the walls above Bishop Gate, along Bishop Street and looking south-west towards the Diamond and the domed Corporation Hall, built in 1784. After the Guildhall was built, this building was for a while a college of art before being burnt down in 1903. It was replaced with floral gardens. The Court House is to the right, while to the left is the imposing town house which was built as the Bishop's Palace in 1753. It remained the residence of the Church of Ireland Bishop until 1945. It was built on the site of an older palace and is now the Freemason's Hall. In 1909 Ephraim Marks opened a penny bazaar in this street. His brother was Michael Marks, a founder of Marks and Spencer.

The Court House was completed in 1817 at a cost of £30,479 and 15 shillings, which included the purchase of the site and furniture. It was designed by Mr John Bowden of Dublin and built of Dungiven sandstone, ornamented with Portland stone. The builders were Henry, Mullens and McMahon, also of Dublin. It measures 126 feet by 66 feet and the façade of a tetra-style Ionic portico was modelled from that of the Temple of Erectheus at Athens. Over the pediment are the royal arms and the wings are surmounted with statues of Justice and Peace, sculptured in Portland stone by Edward Smith. Bishop Gate is at the end of the street.

Right: There has been a St Columb's Cathedral dominating the skyline of the city for nearly four centuries. It was the first Protestant cathedral built in Western Europe after the Reformation and was a fine example of 'Planter's Gothic'. When King James I formed the new County of Londonderry by a Royal Charter in 1613, the Honourable Irish Society in London donated a silver-gilt chalice and paten for a church they hoped would be built. Construction of this church eventually began in 1628 and the spire was made of wood and covered by lead. During repairs some sixty years later the lead, which had been taken down and stored, was used to make cannonballs and bullets during the siege. The foundation stone for the present church was laid on 26 July 1851, but it was not until 4 May 1873 that the cathedral was dedicated by Dr Kelly, Bishop of 'Derry. The spire has a height of 77 metres and a carillon of bells was added in 1902. A granite cross, 2.4 metres high, is on the top of the spire. The gates and a gate lodge were added in 1905.

The Apprentice Boy's Memorial is situated in a corner of the grounds of St Columb's Cathedral close to the city walls. It is dedicated to the thirteen boys who closed the gates of the walls against the advancing armies of King James II in 1688. Sometimes referred to as the Siege Heroes' Mound, it was unveiled on 24 May 1861. There is also an Apprentice Boy's Memorial Hall, which was opened in 1877; an extension to this was built along Society Street in 1937 in memory of the fallen of the First World War.

The Chapter House of St Columb's Cathedral contains many historical items. The room today is more or less exactly the same as in this early photograph. On the right hand side is a most interesting document. It is an agreement made between the citizens of 'Derry, 225 in number, who had suffered loss in the siege, and three of their number – Robert Rockford, David Cairnes MP, and John Maggorth, Town Clerk – promising the citizens up to 1/6th of what compensation the three would receive from the King, Parliament or the Irish Society for damage and loss in the siege. Below the clock is a painting of Cecil Francis Alexander and to its left is her Father Bishop William Alexander, who eventually became the Archbishop of Armagh. The kidney-shaped table in the foreground belonged to Bishop Hervey, Earl of Bristol, who was appointed Bishop in 1768. There was a fire in the Chapter House in 1935, though luckily the contents were carried to safety by parishioners and none were damaged.

Right: Crowds gathering to watch the flames engulf the Guildhall on Easter Sunday, 1908. Only the shell of the building remained and the whole of the interior had to be reconstructed. Built outside the city walls to replace the earlier town hall, which had been situated at the Diamond, the foundation stone of the hall was laid in 1887. Designed by Thomas Grey Ferguson in the Gothic style, it was opened in 1890 at a cost of £20,000. Reconstruction after the fire was completed in 1912 to the drawings of M.A. Robinson. The Council Chamber is laid out in the same style as that of the City of London. The four-faced clock is one of the largest in the British Isles. Unfortunately, the Guildhall was again seriously damaged in June 1972, this time by bombs, but has since been restored to its former glory.

'Roaring Meg' is one of 28 cannons placed around the city walls. These are the best preserved set of seventeenth- and eighteenth-century cannons in the British Isles. The cannon is 11 feet long and has a circumference of four feet, six inches and was donated by the Company of London Fishmongers in 1642. By the style of their dress, the two gentlemen are possibly members of this honourable company, which is still in existence. 'Roaring Meg' was placed in the Double Bastion on the walls, so called because a dividing wall was built in 1689. It is not currently on the walls as it is being restored.

Built in 1865, Magazine Gate is the city's newest gate. At the time of its construction the wall between it and Shipquay gate was raised by two metres and ornamental battlements added. The wall on the left in this view shows the original height. On the keystones on either side of the gate are the carved heads of David Cairns and Col. Adam Murray, two important figures in the siege. On the inside of the gate, in the foreground of this picture, is Magazine Street. Immediately to the left, but out of view, was a large public house, which has since been replaced by the excellent Tower Museum, built in 1982 and opened in 1984. The museum takes its name from the fact that it is housed in a tower and its site was once occupied by a sixteenth-century O'Doherty fort.

Shipquay Place, Londonderry.

Opposite: Shipquay Place looking towards Waterloo Place, busy with many horse-drawn carts and their jarveys awaiting passengers. The fare from here was one shilling for the first mile and eight pence for each additional mile. Along this part of the city walls between Magazine Gate (seen at the end of the wall) and Shipquay Gate, are seven cannon all facing the Guildhall and the river. The first building on the right in Shipquay Place is the impressive Northern Bank, built in 1866 by James Connor. Next is the equally impressive Northern Counties Hotel, built in 1898. The horse-drawn tramway tracks can be seen in the road. The trams were operated by McFarland and took passengers from the Londonderry & Lough Swilly Railway station to the Great Northern station in Foyle Road. 'Derry is the only completely walled city in Ireland. The walls were built under the direction of Thomas Raven to a design of Sir Edward Doddington of Dungiven. Building started in 1613 and was completed in 1618 at a cost of £8,357. The walls were built to protect the new English colonists and to maintain a garrison. Their width varies from 14 to 37 feet and the height varies from 20 to 25 feet; they are 1,710 yards long in total. By 1628 the Irish Society reported that 265 houses had been built within the walls.

Right: The smart uniform on this employee indicates that the Melville Hotel had a certain style. Formerly Jury's Hotel, it was constructed in 1870 by the builder M. McClelland, from a design by the architect C. Sherrie of Belfast, and was situated in Foyle Street at the corner with Orchard Street. The site had previously contained the Army Barracks, built in 1839. It became the Melville Temperance Hotel in 1912 and was renamed the Melville Hotel in 1948. It was a four-storey Georgian-style building and had a large ballroom, which had its own Melville Dance Band. The building was demolished in 1972 after a fire in which two firemen were trapped inside and lost their lives.

A horse-drawn carriage awaits passengers from the Northern Counties Hotel, which also contained the County Café. It was built in 1898. Amelia Earhart breakfasted in this hotel after completing her record-breaking solo flight across the Atlantic in May 1932. She had intended to fly to Paris but was forced to land at Ballyarnett; her flight time was 20 hours, 40 minutes. In the 1930s the hotel advertisements boasted hot and cold water, central heating and 'Zotofoam' baths, and a bus. This magnificent building still stands in Shipquay Place, currently surrounded by scaffolding. It is undergoing complete refurbishment to return it to its former glory thanks to a £2.5 million lottery grant.

Viewed here from Guildhall Square, the City Hotel – built in 1888 – claimed to be 'Derry's leading hotel. An advertisement of the early 1900s stated that it had a principal dining room with seating capacity for 100 with 'cuisine perfect' and the proprietress was Mrs Gibson. It was situated on the corner of Foyle Street and Shipquay Street, adjacent to the Guildhall with views of the city walls and the River Foyle. Unfortunately, it was badly damaged by a bomb and lay in disrepair for a number of years before being demolished in 1972. The site is currently a car park but there are new plans to build a major hotel and retail complex there.

The Imperial Hotel was in Bishop Street and standing outside it in this photograph may well be the proprietor Samuel Nesbitt, late of the Metropole Hotel in Cork. The hotel was built in 1846 by a Mr Greer of Omagh. It consists of three storeys with a Georgian façade. Inside, it had a fine foyer with a double semi-spiral staircase. Prince Albert stayed here when he visited the city in 1869. It was closed by 1914 and was converted to become the shirt factory of A.E. McCandless and Co. The building is now vacant and the railings and porch have gone.

A great view of many modes of transport, including a bus operated by the Londonderry Corporation, on Strand Road looking north-west from Waterloo Place. On the left, with its awning down, are the premises of Hugh Stevenson and Co.; built in 1905, the store had a shop on the ground floor and a restaurant on the first floor. Next door is the large store of T. and J. Smiley and then M. and A. Foster's, advertising luncheons and teas. Many of these fine buildings were destroyed during the 'Troubles' in the early 1970s, although Foster's building still stands surrounded by modern replacements. On the right carts are seen coming out through an arch which led to Victoria Market. The tall building at the end of Strand Road is the Municipal Technical College, built in 1908 and now the North-West Institute of Technology.

Waterloo Place, with Strand Road leading to the north. The tall building on the right, erected in 1906, belonged to G. F. Crook, ladies and gents outfitters, and next door is Maddens' newsagents and confectioners, built in 1904. They also published many local postcards. The 'chemist and druggist' premises, built in 1899, was Glendenning's Medical Hall which sold a perfume called 'The Londonderry Air'. The glass covered building in the centre of Waterloo Place was underground public toilets, which were erected on the site of the 'five lamps' drinking fountain. These were replaced in 1990 by a water feature and a bronze sculpture depicting emigrants escaping the Great Famine.

A view of Brooke Park, in the shadow of the Roman Catholic St Eugene's Cathedral. This is one of the highest points in the city. In 1838 it was decided to build a Catholic cathedral in 'Derry; it cost £40,000 and all the money was collected locally except for £4,000, which came from America. The foundation stone was laid in 1851 and worship began in 1873. The cathedral was designed by J.J. McCarthy of Dublin in a neo-Gothic Style. The nave is 160 feet long and 35 feet wide, while the groined roof is supported by a double series of massive stone pillars. Improvements and additions have been made over the years, the most noticeable being the spire, designed by E.J. Toye of 'Derry and George Ashlin of Dublin. It was built between 1900 and 1903. It is 256 feet tall and topped with a granite cross eight feet in height.

Gwyn's Charitable Institution was founded by Mr John Gwyn. Originally from Muff in Co. Donegal, he was an orphan who later became a merchant in the city. He died in 1823 and left £41,757 specifically for boarding, clothing and educating as many poor boys as the funds would permit. The first institution was opened in April 1833 in a house which had formerly been the City Hotel (not the City Hotel featured on page 23). Later, in 1840, this magnificent building was erected in Brooke Park and was capable of accommodating 200 boys. By 1900 it housed a city museum and later became the municipal library and the headquarters of the Education Committee. It was demolished in 1973 and the foundations are still visible in the park.

A view from above Ferryquay Gate looking down Carlisle Road. This road, which was named after Lord Carlisle, Lord Lieutenant of Ireland, developed after the opening of the Carlisle Bridge in 1863. Several churches were on this road; the one on the left is the neo-Gothic Methodist Church designed by A. Forman of Forman and Aston and built by Colhoun Brothers in 1903. Another was Fourth Derry Presbyterian Church, built in 1877—79. The large building halfway down on the right is the Welch Margetson shirt factory, one of the most impressive industrial edifices of Victorian 'Derry. On the left-hand side just below the church was the Opera House, which opened in 1877 but was burnt down on 9 March 1940.

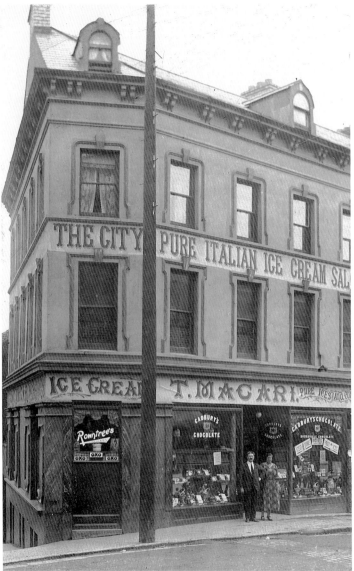

Left: T. Macari's famous Italian ice cream saloon was situated at the top of Carlisle Street at the corner with Bridge Street. The family began the business on William Street. This shop had formerly belonged to J.H. Dunlop and Son who were in the millinery business. Apart from ice cream it is clear that other goods were available: advertised on the windows are Rowntrees, Cadbury and Bourneville chocolate, as well as Oxo. Later, after Macari vacated the building, it became the local labour exchange. The building now has an additional storey and a flat roof, and currently houses a photographic shop.

Right: Carlisle Bridge was built in 1863 at a cost of £100,000. It had a swing bridge centre section and tolls were levied for crossing. The bridge was opened by Lord Carlisle, the Lord Lieutenant of Ireland. Power for the lighting on the bridge was shared between suppliers on either side of the river. On the far side of the river, to the left of the bridge, is the large shirt factory of Tillie and Henderson which was built in 1856 to the design of local architect John Gray Ferguson. A five-storey building covering one acre and consisting of 19,000 square feet, it was said to be the largest shirt factory in the world. Just behind it, on Abercorn Road, is another shirt factory with a distinctive tower (right at the far end of the bridge), which belonged to R. Sinclair and Co.; built in 1863, it was designed by the architect A. McElwee. This factory is still standing while the Tillie and Henderson building has recently been demolished. The central skyline is dominated by the spire of St Columb's Cathedral, while to its right on the skyline the large building with long roof and two turrets is the City and County jail, built in 1781 and demolished in 1971.

Looking west across the Craigavon Bridge from the Waterside, this is a most interesting photograph of the removal of part of the old Carlisle Bridge after its demolition. This dates the photograph to 1933 when Craigavon Bridge was built. This bridge has two decks; the lower was originally used to carry a railway line to shunt goods wagons between the stations, but is now a single standard carriageway opened for road use in 1968. The bridge was named after James Craig, Lord Craigavon, the first Prime Minister of Northern Ireland, and was built alongside the old Carlisle Bridge; from March to July 1933 both bridges operated alongside one another. On the right above the Foyle Street railway station is the Opera House.

The Londonderry & Coleraine Railway was the other railway built from the city on the 1840s; it operated to Coleraine from this station on the Waterside and was later extended to Belfast. The GNR(I) line to Omagh and Enniskillen operated from a city side station on Foyle Street. In 1863 the Londonderry & Lough Swilly Railway was opened, running to Buncrana in Co. Donegal. The fourth railway from Londonderry ran from Victoria Road Station to Strabane and was operated by the London Midland Scottish Railway. The clock tower of this building was completed to the design of John Lanyon in 1863. The initials of the original company, the Belfast & Northern Counties Railway, surmount the portal. While the front has been modified, the building is still intact.

During the Great Famine of the 1840s two railways were built from 'Derry. One of these was the Londonderry & Enniskillen Railway, which was built to Omagh and then to Enniskillen. It later joined up with the lines to Belfast and Dublin at Portadown and it became part of the Great Northern Railway. Shown here is part of the goods depot south of the Foyle Road Station on the river's edge at Collins Strand. The Star shirt factory can be seen in the background.

The Carlisle Bridge, as viewed from the Waterside, was constructed in 1863 to replace an earlier wooden bridge which had been built by Cox and Thompson and Co. in Boston in the United States. It was transported and positioned in the Bridge Street area, just north of the site of the present Craigavon Bridge. The first bridge across the Foyle had been constructed in 1791 at a cost of £16,294. It was badly damaged by floating ice in 1814 and replaced at a cost of £18,300. The Carlisle Bridge, which cost £100,000, had a centre portion which could be swivelled ninety degrees to permit upstream navigation. The lower deck carried standard gauge track, thus linking the BNCR terminus on the Waterside, which can be seen in the foreground, with the Great Northern Railways (Ireland) terminus at Foyle Road, which has the arched windows on the city side of the water. The wagons in the foreground belong to the County Donegal Railway.

The Londonderry Model School was situated on an elevated three-acre site at Northland Road. Although it was replaced in 1962 by a new building (currently the Londonderry Primary School), the gates and pillars of the model school are still intact, along with the small gate lodge to the left of the entrance. The first model schools were designed in the nineteenth century by the Board of National Education, headed by Frederick Darley. In 1856, at about the time of Jacob Owen's retirement as architect to the National Board of Public Works and the appointment of his son, James H. Owen, as his successor, it was decided to transfer responsibility for school design to Public Works, phasing out Darley's department. J.H. Owen's design for the Londonderry Model was completed in 1860. The design was for two wings with a corridor along the back of the building connecting the teaching rooms. In this building the most significant room was the boy's schoolroom. Apparently intended for 250 boys, it measured 50 feet by 40 feet, a space containing 24 desks in two parallel rows separated by four columns of a massive Gothic arcade. The school also had a classroom devoted to maritime studies, recognition of the fact that the city was an important northern port. The school was built by Boyd's Contractors and was opened on 13 January 1862 by the Rt. Rev. William Higgin MA DD, Lord Bishop of Londonderry and Raphoe. Its importance was recognised when it was inspected by the Earl of Carlisle, Lord Lieutenant of Ireland on the 25 September 1863 (he opened the Carlisle Bridge on the same day). The school was transferred to the Londonderry County Borough Education Authority on 1 April 1929 and was rebuilt and enlarged during 1935—38.

Girls of Londonderry High School playing hockey in the grounds of 'Duncreggan'. The school owes its existence to the merging of two independent institutions. The first of these, the Ladies' Collegiate School, was set up in 1877 at No. 11 Queen Street by the Misses McKillop, pioneers in the movement for higher education for women in Ireland. The school later moved to Crawford Square and was renamed Victoria High School, taking in both boarders and day pupils. The other school, at the top of Lawrence Hill, was St Lurach's College, opened by Miss J. Kerr around 1900. When Strand House School (established in 1860) closed during the First World War, its girls mostly went to Victoria or St Lurach's and these amalgamated in 1922 to form Londonderry High School. In 1928 the school purchased and moved to 'Duncreggan' which was formerly the home of the local industrialist and shirt manufacturer William Tillie. He built it in 1870 and lived there until the 1930s. It is now the premises of the senior school of Foyle and Londonderry College which was created when Foyle College and Londonderry High School merged in 1976.

Foyle College traces its roots to the original Diocesan school founded within the city walls as a free grammar school in the reign of King James I. It was rebuilt on a site outside the walls to the north of the city in 1814 and was renamed Foyle College. The game of rugby has always been popular in the school, its teams winning the Ulster Schools Cup twice, first in 1900, beating Methodist College, and in 1915, beating the Royal School, Armagh. This is the school's 1st rugby XV, photographed in 1928/29. The captain, who is holding the ball, is B.M. Smith and he also played for Ulster as signified by the red hand on his jersey.

Back row (from left): Dr Layng, J.H. Brewster, A.M. Langtry, R.M. Warnock, J.M. Moore. S.G. Gourley, R.H. Beattie, J. Truesdale, F.R. O'Neill, BA;
Middle row: K. Gregg, W.H. Kerr, W.L. Hazlett, B.M. Smith (captain), B.McC. Jamieson, J.C.P. Black, J.E.A. Thompson;
Front row: B.A. Bovaird, A.M.H. Simmons, A. McDonald, W. Huey.

The Waterside, as viewed from the city side piers on the west bank. Several large churches dominate the skyline of the city and to the left is the Parish of Clooney All Saints Church of Ireland. This church was planned by Bishop Higgin and built on a site donated by James Murray of Caw. The architect was W.H. Lynn of Belfast and the builder was A. McElwee. It is in the neo-Gothic style and fits into a difficult corner site with sloping ground. Its first rector was the Rev. John Russell, followed by Rev. J.A. Stewart, who was responsible for the building of the Stewart Memorial Hall, now the Stewart Memorial School. With the building of the Carlisle Bridge in 1863 and the expansion of the city to the Waterside there was demand for more churches. The Waterside Presbyterian church to the right was built between 1864 and 1865, while just below it is the Reformed Presbyterian Church. The Belfast & Northern Counties Railway line runs along the side of the river.

A photograph of the River Foyle taken from high up on the Waterside, the east bank of the River Foyle. This sweep of the river contained the various quays that made up the port, and in those days there were quays on both banks. On the Waterside these were replaced by the Foyle Embankment, while on the east bank the quays and many buildings were removed to provide the dual traffic flow on Duke Street. In the picture, alongside the Abercorn quay are eight Flower Class corvettes which were used as escort vessels for convoys during the Second World War.

A view of Ebrington Barracks on the Waterside, as viewed from the Guildhall around 1907. The army barracks were originally situated in Foyle Street, on a site which became the Melville Hotel, and were built for a regiment of the infantry in 1839. They were replaced by these barracks, named after the Viscount Ebrington who was Lord Lieutenant of Ireland. The move across the river was strongly opposed but led to a rapid expansion of the city on the Waterside. Changes and additions were made to the barracks over the years. During the Second World War the barracks became HMS Sea Eagle and a joint Royal Navy/Royal Air Force anti-submarine school was established in 1940, remaining until 1970. The barracks were handed back to the British Army who vacated them at the start of 2005, and they are now available for development.

The Permanent Staff of the Royal Garrison Artillery (Militia), pictured outside Ebrington Barracks in 1907. Queen Elizabeth I had established a garrison on the hill above the River Foyle as early as 1566. Two bugle boys are lying on the grass. The sergeant-major and the senior officer, either a captain or a major, are wearing peaked caps, while the rest are wearing a type of headgear known as 'brodericks'. These were named after William St John Broderick, Secretary of State for War from 1900 to 1903, who was responsible for their introduction. They did not last long in service. All uniforms, other than the officer's, have the elaborate Austrian knot on the forearm. Rank badges of the NCOs are worn on the upper arm, while the sergeant-major's rank badge, a crown, is worn on the forearm above the knot. Some of the men are wearing trade or qualification badges and a few are wearing good conduct badges, which are inverted chevrons on the right forearm. A few are also wearing medals which at this time probably indicated service in the South African War.

A view north of the actual commercial area of the port, the steps out of the water led to the City of 'Derry Boating Club. One of the oldest rowing clubs in the world, it was founded in 1860. Their clubhouse (fitted with a gymnasium in 1874), at the bottom of Boating Club Lane, was the building with the tower to the right of the chimneys. As part of the Foyle Embankment scheme it has been restored recently and is the Quaywest restaurant and wine bar; the club itself is now based at the present boat house on the Waterside. The taller chimney is the coal-fired power station for the Londonderry Electricity company. The building on the far right is the Municipal Technical College, now the North-West Institute of Technology.

A large sailing ship is alongside the Queen's Quay just north of the Guildhall. It could be an 'ice-ship' because at this time ice was imported from Norway and Greenland. The large five-storey building is McCorkell's grain mill. The small boats belonged to the City of 'Derry Boating Club. More than 200,000 emigrants left from the quays at 'Derry in the first 70 years of the nineteenth century – many as a result of the Great Famine – seeking a better life in the United States of America. The southern part of the quays was covered over with the building of the Foyle Embankment in 1975, while the northern part was reclaimed in 1995 to provide building land.

This postcard was one from a book of cards sold by A.E. Dickson, a chemist in the city. The book was entitled 'Surrender' and depicted the surrender of German U-boats at Lisahally. The Prime Minister of Northern Ireland, Sir Basil Brooke, attended the ceremony on 14 May 1945 along with Admiral Sir Maxwell Horton, Commander in Chief of the Western Approaches. Lisahally was a submarine base on the River Foyle, just to the north of the city. At that time it was commanded by Commander Philip Francis, who was responsible for managing the berthing of the companies of the 63 U-boats that surrendered there. He reported that he was tremendously impressed with the German submariners' discipline and impeccable conduct in the aftermath of enormous losses and final defeat. These U-boats, numbers 1305, 1005, 1058 and 1009, along with 59 others, were taken to deep water off Lough Foyle and scuttled as part of Operation Deadlight from 25 November 1945 until 15 February 1946. The piers to the right are now the site for the new deep-water port of Londonderry Port and Harbour Commissioners, built in 1995.

A view of the aerodrome at Eglinton, Co. 'Derry, in 1935. During the Second World War it was one of three aerodromes in the north-west of Northern Ireland used to provide air cover for the North Atlantic Fleet. It was a Royal Fleet Air Arm base and was used by American and British airmen. Known as HMS Gannet, it was closed down in 1959, but partially reopened in 1966 as HMS Eagle. It later became the home for the Eglinton Flying Club, which maintained the site, and in 1978 'Derry City Council purchased it and 'Derry City Airport was opened. Despite some financial difficulties, the airport has scheduled services to a number of UK airports as well as to Dublin and currently deals with 22,000 passengers per year. The aircraft in the photograph is a Miles Mark 2, designed by Mr and Mrs Miles, well-known aircraft designers and constructors, and built by Philips and Powis Aircraft Ltd in 1934 and registered in 1935.

Rodgers and Co. were large general drapers situated at No. 13 the Diamond. This later became the shop of Johnston and Flynn, outfitters, and is now occupied by the HSBC bank.

Professor H. A. Tipper, Champion world weight carrier, and on his Bicycle, drew 2 Ladies and a Sulky at Royal Sydney Show, 1905, also 8 hours sports, 1904, witnessed by 50,000

Prof. H. A. Tipper 6ft. 2in' 14 stone. World's Champion Cyclist from Australian Bush, and his worl champion Bicycles BUILT BY HIMSELF which he rides. The 10in. bicycle. 12lbs, carried two men 386lbs, or 27 stone at Lunkalk, Londonderry, also Bristol. No Wager

TOURING ROUND THE WORLD, so far 32.800 Miles H. A. TIPPER carried 103lbs. weight ½ mile. Time 1min. 10 sec Special Prizes 1904-5-6 Sydney and Melbourne, Victoria where he was born.

This is Professor H.A. Tipper, who was born in Melbourne, Australia, in 1867. He was known as the 'wonderful man' and was an inventor, bicycle rider, and 'self-taught engineer'. In 1887 he began riding a bicycle around the world. In 1908 he claimed that he had left Australia with one penny, earning his living by riding the 'smallest bicycle in the world'. Having cycled 33,900 miles, he returned to Australia in 1924 with four shillings and sixpence. During these travels he visited 'Derry, where he carried two men, with a combined weight of 27 stone, on his ten-inch bicycle. In 1924 he travelled in a motor car steered by a horse for a total of 85,000 miles. Definitely an eccentric!